SUMMARY OF CRITICAL MASS

Ignite the Holy Fire of Revival that Transforms You into a Supernatural Warrior

MARIO MURILLO

DESTINY IMAGE

All emphasis within Scripture quotations is the author's own. Please note that Destiny Image's publishing style capitalizes certain pronouns in Scripture that refer to the Father, Son, and Holy Spirit, and may differ from some publishers' styles. Take note that the name satan and related names are not capitalized. We choose not to acknowledge him, even to the point of violating grammatical rules.

Destiny Image P.O. Box 310, Shippensburg, PA 17257-0310

This book and all other Destiny Image's books are available at Christian bookstores and distributors worldwide.

For Worldwide Distribution.

Reach us on the Internet: www.destinyimage.com.

ISBN 13 TP: 9798881500344

ISBN 13 eBook: 9798881500351

CONTENTS

Introduction v

1. Stage One: God Seeks a Core 1
2. Stage Two: The Attitude That Gains Entrance 5
3. Stage Three: The Birthing Prayer 9
4. Stage Four: Critical Mass 13
5. Stage Five: The Dark Night of the Soul 17
6. Stage Six: The Steel Punch of God 21
7. Stage Seven: Making Revival Permanent 25

About the Publisher 29

INTRODUCTION

Introduction to the Summary of "Critical Mass"

In the profound exploration of "Critical Mass," we delve into the pivotal juncture where the accumulated spiritual fervor of believers reaches a transformative breaking point, akin to a nuclear reaction in the realm of faith. This chapter is not just an analysis; it's a compelling narrative that unfolds the tremendous potential that lies within concerted and sincere prayer, unified community action, and divine empowerment. As we dissect the processes and divine mechanics behind this spiritual phenomenon, we come to understand how pivotal moments in scriptural and contemporary Christian history have hinged upon reaching this critical mass.

The concept of "Critical Mass" in a spiritual context is drawn from the dramatic events that unfolded in the Upper Room in Jerusalem, where 120 believers, through their unified and persistent intercession, received the Holy Spirit. This moment was not merely a historical event but a template for how God's power can radically transform society through His people today. The essence of this chapter is to convey that while the arrival of the Holy Spirit on Pentecost was a unique event, the principle behind it—a divine empowerment following a concentrated spiritual buildup—is repeatable and essential for the church's mission in the modern world.

Through this summary, readers will be invited to reflect on the dynamic truth that the power of God is unleashed in spectacular measure when His people align in purpose and prayer. The aim is to illuminate the path back to spiritual power for today's church, which often finds itself entangled in mediocrity and ineffectiveness. By revisiting the scriptural accounts and historical awakenings, this summary serves as a clarion call for believers to reconvene in their "Upper Rooms," seeking God with a renewed fervor and anticipation of the "Critical Mass" that can once again turn the tide in favor of the Kingdom.

Thus, this introduction sets the stage for a journey through the "Critical Mass" chapter, promising readers an insightful, inspiring, and transformative experience. It challenges each one to participate actively in the divine equation that promises not only to revive but to sustain a move of God that can sweep across lands and generations. The summary underscores the significance of each believer's role in this divine synergy and encourages a commitment to the spiritual disciplines that foster such powerful outcomes.

CHAPTER 1

STAGE ONE: GOD SEEKS A CORE

Bible Verse

"If My people who are called by My name will humble themselves, and pray and seek My face, and turn from their wicked ways, then I will hear from heaven, and will forgive their sin and heal their land." — 2 Chronicles 7:14

Introduction

In this impassioned chapter, the author emphasizes the profound impact a dedicated group of believers can have on society. By invoking the powerful potential of collective, focused prayer and righteous action, he argues that even a small number of faithful individuals can bring about significant spiritual revival and transformation within their communities and beyond.

Word of Wisdom

"God's decision to spare a nation is

based upon finding and purifying His people. The depravity of our country should not preoccupy our thinking." Mario Murillo

Main Theme

The main theme centers on the transformative power of a committed group of believers, termed a "revival core," whose dedication to God's purposes can lead to substantial changes not just within the church, but across nations and societies.

Key Points

- A small, devoted group can wield enormous influence and bring about societal revival.
- The secular world advances with dedication, lacking the gospel's power, highlighting a missed opportunity for believers.
- True transformation in society begins with personal and collective repentance and dedicated prayer.
- The fate of nations can hinge on the righteousness and intercession of God's people.
- Believers are called to focus not on material acquisitions but on significant spiritual victories.
- Establishing a core of devout followers is the first critical step toward initiating widespread spiritual revival.

Key Themes

- **The Power of Few**: The author illustrates how historically, significant changes have often been initiated by a small number of people. This principle applies spiritually as well, where even a handful of committed believers can set the stage for massive revival.
- **Secular vs. Spiritual Achievement**: Highlighting examples like Facebook and Twitter, the author laments the church's comparative lack of impact, suggesting that believers have the potential to achieve even more if they harness their spiritual authority with as much vigor as secular innovators do their resources.
- **Role of Righteousness**: The biblical story of Abraham negotiating with God over Sodom and Gomorrah underscores the significant role that righteousness plays in God's decision-making about a nation, reinforcing the need for a righteous "core" within the city.
- **Revival Over Comfort**: The author criticizes the modern church's focus on building physical monuments rather than fostering spiritual growth and outreach. He calls for resources to be directed towards empowering believers and impacting lives beyond the church walls.
- **Identity and Authority**: By embracing their identity as God's chosen and understanding the authority that comes with it, believers can confidently face and influence their societies. This self-

realization is crucial for effective spiritual leadership and revival.

Conclusion

The chapter concludes by urging believers to recognize their potential and responsibility to affect divine change. By forming a committed core that seeks God's face and stands for His righteousness, they can hope to see a revival that not only preserves but profoundly transforms their societies. The author calls for a return to genuine, powerful engagement with God, which holds the promise of divine intervention in desperate times.

CHAPTER 2

STAGE TWO: THE ATTITUDE THAT GAINS ENTRANCE

Bible Verse

"If My people who are called by My name will humble themselves, and pray and seek My face, and turn from their wicked ways, then I will hear from heaven, and will forgive their sin and heal their land." — 2 Chronicles 7:14

Introduction

This chapter delves into the profound spiritual discipline required to effectively engage with God for national revival. The author emphasizes that mere desire is insufficient; a specific, humble posture before God is necessary to gain the divine momentum needed to bring about significant change.

Word of Wisdom

"You stand before the greatest door in history. Beyond this door lie the most precious gifts of God." Mario Murillo

Main Theme

The chapter explores the critical attitudes and preparations necessary for believers to effectively seek and facilitate a revival, stressing the importance of humility, repentance, and a profound commitment to God's will.

Key Points

- True humility is essential for accessing God's power and initiating revival.
- Effective prayer for revival requires a clear understanding and removal of personal and communal hindrances.
- God's invitation to revival demands a response that goes beyond superficial engagement.
- Preparation for revival must involve practical readiness and spiritual purification.
- True revival impacts beyond the church walls, aiming for societal transformation.

Key Themes

- **Humility and Recognition of Need**: The initial step towards genuine revival is recognizing and deeply feeling the current spiritual poverty and societal decay. This humility opens the door to meaningful intercession and divine intervention.

- **Preparation Beyond Prayer**: It's not enough to simply pray for revival; believers must prepare their hearts and communities for the changes it will bring. This includes setting aside personal agendas and making practical preparations for accommodating a movement of God.
- **Confronting and Casting Off Sin**: The integrity of one's prayer life and their effectiveness in seeking revival is directly impacted by personal purity. Actively addressing and repenting from sin is portrayed as a non-negotiable precursor to standing in the gap for a nation.
- **Community and Leadership in Revival**: The role of church leaders is critically examined, with a call for them to prioritize spiritual vitality over numerical growth. Leaders are encouraged to foster a culture of deep spiritual commitment and readiness for revival.
- **The Necessity of Spiritual Vigor**: The final readiness for revival involves a vibrant, expectant faith that actively prepares for the outcomes of prayer. This includes equipping believers to handle an influx of spiritual growth and societal impact, ensuring the church is a well-prepared vessel for revival.

Conclusion

The chapter concludes with a powerful call to action for believers to approach God with a correct attitude, fully prepared and expecting Him to move mightily. The author emphasizes that entering into a phase of revival is both a privilege and a responsibility, requiring a committed, cleansed, and unified body of believers ready to be used by God for His transformative purposes.

CHAPTER 3

STAGE THREE: THE BIRTHING PRAYER

Bible Verse

"If My people who are called by My name will humble themselves, and pray and seek My face, and turn from their wicked ways, then I will hear from heaven, and will forgive their sin and heal their land." — 2 Chronicles 7:14

Introduction

This chapter vividly describes the intense, transformative prayer experience of the author, which leads to personal revival and community transformation. It emphasizes the profound spiritual commitment required to bring about significant change through prayer.

Word of Wisdom

"The power of Satan in this city has been pierced tonight. Now you will see a

breakthrough. I have given you this city."
Mario Murillo

Main Theme

The main theme of the chapter focuses on "travailing prayer," a deep, intense form of intercession that mirrors the emotional and spiritual intensity of childbirth, which the author equates to the process necessary for birthing a revival in a community or city.

Key Points

- Intense personal crisis can trigger profound spiritual encounters and commitments.
- True intercessory prayer can be emotionally and physically overwhelming but is necessary for spiritual breakthroughs.
- Prayer is not just asking God for things; it is a deep spiritual battle against principalities and powers.
- Spiritual victories are often preceded by intense spiritual warfare.
- Revival in a community can start with a single committed individual.
- True intercessory prayer involves complete spiritual and emotional investment.

Key Themes

- **Intensity and Commitment of Intercessory Prayer**: The author's personal story of praying through the night illustrates the depth of commitment and emotional intensity required for what he calls "birthing prayer." This type of prayer goes beyond casual requests to a deep, labor-like process involving the whole being.
- **Spiritual Warfare and Community Impact**: The narrative connects intense prayer with tangible changes in the community, suggesting that such prayers have the power to break spiritual strongholds and bring about revival. It emphasizes that prayer is both a personal struggle and a communal weapon.
- **Preparation and Participation in Revival**: The author suggests that personal preparation and purity are necessary for effective intercession. He underscores the importance of being spiritually and morally prepared to stand in the gap for others.
- **Empathy and Identification with the Burden**: Identifying deeply with the spiritual and moral state of one's community is essential for effective intercessory prayer. The author's transformation from despair to dedication highlights how personal revival can lead to community transformation.
- **The Role of Divine Encounters in Prayer**: The chapter highlights the

mysterious and often supernatural aspects of deep prayer, including potential angelic encounters and direct messages from God. These experiences empower the intercessor and confirm their role in God's plan for revival.

Conclusion

The chapter concludes by reinforcing the power and necessity of intercessory prayer in the life of a believer who seeks not only personal transformation but also desires to impact their community profoundly. It calls believers to a higher level of spiritual engagement, marked by sacrifice, intensity, and a commitment to fight spiritual battles through prayer.

CHAPTER 4

STAGE FOUR: CRITICAL MASS

Bible Verse

"If My people who are called by My name will humble themselves, and pray and seek My face, and turn from their wicked ways, then I will hear from heaven, and will forgive their sin and heal their land." — 2 Chronicles 7:14

Introduction

This chapter delves into the concept of "critical mass" in the spiritual realm, drawing parallels between nuclear fission and the empowering of believers to effect dramatic change. It reflects on the historic moment in the Upper Room in Jerusalem and the transformative power of the Holy Spirit.

Word of Wisdom

"The glory will come; sin will be cleansed. Soon it will start intensifying.

Barriers will be broken until suddenly—bang!—tongues of fire." Mario Murillo

Main Theme

The main theme is about reaching a "critical mass" in spiritual terms where collective, intense prayer and unity among believers trigger a powerful movement of the Holy Spirit, reminiscent of the Pentecost, leading to widespread revival and transformation.

Key Points

• The Upper Room in Jerusalem is the historical backdrop where believers reached a critical mass.

• True spiritual power requires a group of believers reaching a state of readiness and purity.

• The concept of critical mass is compared to nuclear fission, emphasizing the need for a small but pure group to initiate significant change.

• Historical revivals led by figures like Martin Luther and John Wesley showcased the power of reaching critical mass.

• Modern believers must seek a return to this form of spiritual potency to impact the world meaningfully.

Key Themes

- **Historical Context and Modern Parallel**: Reflecting on the Pentecost, the author uses this historical event as a blueprint for modern-day believers, advocating for a return to genuine, fervent prayer and spiritual empowerment to fulfill God's commission.

- **Spiritual Dynamics of Revival**: The process of reaching critical mass involves intense spiritual purification and unity among believers, akin to the conditions necessary for nuclear fission, where a significant spiritual breakthrough can only occur with the right conditions.
- **Challenges and Commitment**: The author challenges the modern church to recognize its failures in spiritual potency and calls for a radical return to the principles that fueled early church growth and power, emphasizing humility and dependency on the Holy Spirit.
- **The Role of the Holy Spirit in Empowering Believers**: The empowerment of believers through the Holy Spirit is central to achieving critical mass; this divine empowerment is necessary to overcome the spiritual inertia that hinders church effectiveness.
- **Unity and Purity in the Church**: The need for unity and purity among believers is stressed as essential for reaching critical mass. The church is called to focus on spiritual depth and power rather than external growth and acceptance.

Conclusion

The chapter concludes with a compelling call to action for believers to seek the Holy Spirit's fullness through deep, committed prayer and unity. This pursuit of critical mass is portrayed not just as beneficial but essential for overcoming spiritual malaise and igniting a powerful revival that can transform societies. The author insists that this intense spiritual engagement is the key to unlocking divine power and fulfilling the church's mission on Earth.

CHAPTER 5

STAGE FIVE: THE DARK NIGHT OF THE SOUL

Bible Verse

"If My people who are called by My name will humble themselves, and pray and seek My face, and turn from their wicked ways, then I will hear from heaven, and will forgive their sin and heal their land." — 2 Chronicles 7:14

Introduction

This chapter explores the challenging phase in spiritual growth and revival preparation known as the "dark night of the soul," likened to a moment right before nuclear fission where everything appears to stall, and the potential for significant spiritual breakthrough is at its peak.

Word of Wisdom

"At no other point does God express love more than when He allows this time of total emptiness." Mario Murillo

Main Theme

The theme focuses on enduring through the spiritual desolation of the dark night of the soul, where believers feel abandoned by God. This phase is crucial for purification and preparation for a powerful revival.

Key Points

• Believers may experience a profound spiritual drought known as the dark night of the soul.

• This phase is a testing ground for faith, where apparent abandonment leads to deeper spiritual commitment.

• The dark night is necessary to prepare and purify believers for substantial roles in spiritual revival.

• Just as scientists increase their efforts when close to breakthrough, believers must intensify their prayers during spiritual dryness.

• Persevering through this dark night can lead to a powerful spiritual renewal and significant revival.

Key Themes

- **Testing Faith and Perseverance**: The dark night of the soul tests the believer's faith and perseverance, crucial for preparing them to handle both divine blessings and satanic attacks. This phase ensures that only those truly dedicated and purified will lead and sustain a revival.

- **Spiritual Purification Beyond Sin**: Beyond repenting for actions, the dark night of the soul purifies believers at a deeper level, refining their spiritual 'ways' or innate character. This purification aligns them more closely with God's will and ways, beyond mere acts of faith.
- **Necessity of Spiritual Desolation**: This spiritual desolation is deemed necessary by God to cultivate humility and reliance solely on Him, stripping away self-reliance and superficial faith. It reveals true motives and dedication to God's cause.
- **Parallel to Physical Phenomena**: Drawing parallels between spiritual experiences and nuclear physics, the chapter explains how critical breakthroughs often follow intense pressure and apparent setbacks, illustrating how spiritual empowerment can similarly follow intense spiritual struggle.
- **Outcome of Perseverance**: For those who endure through this dark phase, the promise is a revival marked by God's manifest presence and power. The transformation from despair to dynamism mirrors the explosive power of nuclear fission, signifying a rapid and vast spread of spiritual revival.

Conclusion

The chapter concludes by emphasizing the transformative potential of enduring the dark night of the soul. It challenges believers to persist in their spiritual commitments, promising that such endurance leads to profound spiritual renewal and widespread revival, marked by the evident move of God's Spirit.

CHAPTER 6

STAGE SIX: THE STEEL PUNCH OF GOD

Bible Verse

"If My people who are called by My name will humble themselves, and pray and seek My face, and turn from their wicked ways, then I will hear from heaven, and will forgive their sin and heal their land." — 2 Chronicles 7:14

Introduction

The chapter discusses the dramatic and transformative impact of revival, likened to a "Steel Punch," where collective prayer and divine intervention penetrate spiritual barriers, leading to profound changes in communities and individuals.

Word of Wisdom

"Our prayers and worship do affect God, they do arm angels, and they do release the Holy Spirit. Once more Satan

will be forced to suffer the consequences of the cross: a fresh Steel Punch of God!"
Mario Murillo

Main Theme

The concept of the "Steel Punch of God" is explored as a powerful, sudden movement of God in response to fervent prayer, which disrupts and overcomes spiritual strongholds much like a decisive military tactic overcomes physical barriers.

Key Points

- Revival is compared to a sudden and forceful military tactic, known as the "Steel Punch."
- Historical examples of dramatic spiritual breakthroughs illustrate the concept.
- Persistence in prayer, even during the darkest times, leads to spiritual victories.
- The power of collective prayer is emphasized as a tool for overcoming great spiritual challenges.
- Understanding the full implications of the cross is essential to harnessing this spiritual power.

Key Themes

- **Historical and Biblical Parallels**: The chapter draws parallels between biblical events and modern revival stories to illustrate how dramatic interventions from God have historically changed the course of entire communities, similar to how Israel's military tactics overcame physical barriers.
- **The Nature of Spiritual Warfare**: It discusses the intense spiritual warfare involved in revival, describing the preparation, the challenges faced, and the eventual breakthrough that comes after persistent, faith-filled prayer, emphasizing that this breakthrough is akin to overcoming heavily fortified barriers.
- **Role of Divine Empowerment**: The necessity of divine empowerment through the Holy Spirit is highlighted, detailing how this power is essential for the church to overcome satanic strongholds and bring about widespread revival.
- **Impact of Collective Prayer**: The effect of unified, fervent prayer by a committed group within the church is described as creating a 'force field' of spiritual conviction and transformation that can affect even those not directly involved in the prayer efforts.
- **Transformation Through Trial**: The chapter underscores that significant spiritual breakthroughs often follow intense spiritual trials, described as the

'dark night of the soul,' which test the faith and resolve of those seeking revival.

Conclusion

This chapter concludes with a call to understand and engage in the kind of deep, persistent prayer that leads to significant spiritual breakthroughs. It encourages believers to view their intercessory efforts as critical battles in spiritual warfare, capable of bringing about the "Steel Punch of God" that can transform societies and heal lands according to the promise of 2 Chronicles 7:14.

CHAPTER 7
STAGE SEVEN: MAKING REVIVAL PERMANENT

Bible Verse

"If My people who are called by My name will humble themselves, and pray and seek My face, and turn from their wicked ways, then I will hear from heaven, and will forgive their sin and heal their land." — 2 Chronicles 7:14

Introduction

This chapter discusses the crucial transition from experiencing a temporary revival to establishing it as a continuous and enduring movement, emphasizing the challenges and strategies necessary for making revival a sustained reality.

Word of Wisdom

"Revival is not fragile! It doesn't simply evaporate." Mario Murillo

Main Theme

The chapter explores the concept of transitioning from a temporary revival, characterized by the "Steel Punch of God," to a sustainable movement that permanently transforms individuals and communities.

Key Points

• The immediate effects of revival can be thrilling, but they pose the risk of leading to extreme and unsustainable practices.

• True revival should integrate into daily living, impacting every aspect of life.

• Ensuring revival's permanence requires a disciplined continuation of practices that led to the revival.

• The community transformed by revival must turn its attention to practical, long-term applications.

• Maintenance of revival involves strategic planning and community involvement to address both spiritual and societal needs.

Key Themes

- **Sustainable Practices**: The transition from revival to routine requires the establishment of sustainable spiritual practices that integrate the principles of revival into daily life. This includes fostering environments where the excitement of revival is balanced with the responsibility of maintaining spiritual health and community welfare.

- **Community Transformation**: A permanent revival impacts not only individual lives but also the broader community, requiring ongoing efforts in discipleship, service, and engagement. The chapter emphasizes the need for the church to become a beacon of hope and practical help, continuously reaching out and addressing societal needs.
- **Spiritual and Social Balance**: The excitement of revival must not detract from the responsibilities of daily life and societal obligations. The true measure of revival's success is its ability to enhance rather than detract from responsibilities like work, education, and family.
- **Holistic Gospel Approach**: Revival should promote a holistic approach to Christianity that includes fervent spirituality, robust community service, and active engagement in societal issues. This balanced approach ensures that the revival is not just a series of emotional experiences but a deep, transformative movement that affects all areas of life.
- **Guarding Against Extremes**: The chapter warns against the dangers of emotionalism and extremism, which can discredit the revival in the public eye. It calls for a mature, balanced approach to maintaining the fervor without burning out or veering into fanaticism.

Conclusion

The chapter concludes by underscoring the necessity of making revival a permanent fixture in the life of the church and its community. It challenges believers to continue the disciplines that fostered revival and to integrate these practices into a continuous lifestyle that honors God and effectively ministers to the world. This involves a commitment to spiritual growth, community service, and an ongoing embrace of the transformative power of revival.

DESTINY IMAGE

Destiny Image is a prophetic Christian publisher dedicated to empowering believers through Spirit-led messages. Our mission is to equip and inspire individuals to fulfill their God-given destinies by providing transformative resources that resonate with the Charismatic and Pentecostal faith.

We specialize in books, blogs, and back cover copies that reflect prophetic insights, dynamic teachings, and testimonies of faith. Our commitment to fostering spiritual growth and kingdom impact makes Destiny Image a beacon for those seeking to deepen their relationship with God and embrace their calling in the power of the Holy Spirit.

www.ingramcontent.com/pod-product-compliance
Lightning Source LLC
Chambersburg PA
CBHW052136150726
48002CB00006B/2633

* 9 7 9 8 8 8 1 5 0 0 3 4 4 *